STILL GROWING

B. L. SCOTT

AMENISM, INC.
Fremont, California

Still Growing
by B. L. Scott

Published by Amenism, Inc.
35640 Fremont Blvd #143
Fremont, CA 94536

Copyright © 2025 by Brenda Lorraine Scott

All rights reserved. No part of this publication may be reproduced, stored in a retrieval system, or transmitted in any form, or by any means electronic, mechanical, photocopying, recording, or otherwise, without the written permission of the author and the publisher.

On the cover: The baobab tree, also known as the Tree of Life. Photographer: Eugen Haag

Cover design: Tiyo Karenga and Tarík Karenga

ISBN 978-0-9669742-1-8

CONTENTS

	FOREWORD	vii
1	And My Heart Is Dancing Alone	1
2	Baby Boy	5
3	Blue Star Blessing	7
4	Gone Fish'n	9
5	He's the One	11
6	I Am	13
7	Just Because	15
8	Just Call Me Scott	17
9	Kissing	19
10	Libation for Our Ancestors	21
11	Little Sister	25
12	My Life Revolves Around Me	29
13	Perfect	33
14	Real Black Men	35

15	Revelations of a Stolen Child	39
16	She Is	43
17	So What	45
18	Strong Black Woman	47
19	Thankful	51
20	The Love Up In Here	53
21	Time to Be	57

FOREWORD

For a number of years, my three children urged me to write a book chronicling my life. This book of poetry, although I'm sure it's not what they envisioned, is the realization of their desire. Therefore, I dedicate this effort to the three loves of my life: Thanayi Anana, Tiyo Siyolo and Tarik Saidi. I love each of you, collectively and individually. May you always walk and live in truth!

1

AND MY HEART IS DANCING ALONE

***Today is Wednesday, March, 19, 2008
and It's Been Exactly One Year Today***

It's been one year now
and my heart is still broken...
this time he's gone for good
With the passing of time, I can say,
I no longer cry every day—
just almost every day

It's for real; it's definitely no bad dream;
he's gone away... For the second time
and my heart is dancing alone

Even though he wasn't my first love...
and I'm sure he won't be my last,
He was my forever love, my soul's mate,
my rock, my flame
He's the one who was supposed to stay...
I'm the one I thought would be gone away

What a cruel turn for life to take...
leaving me standing in the middle of the floor
My heart dancing alone, again

STILL GROWING

We first met over thirty years ago…
on a quiet southern summer eve
I was where I shouldn't be…
when a voice reached through the darkness
and rescued me

Captivating my mind… enchanting my soul…
communicating with a glance
Waltzing away with my heart…
in a never ending dance

Ours was not a lusty, hot and steamy,
I want your body kind of love
Rather, it was an all consuming,
I want to share your world kind of love
And for a time we danced, lost in each other,
caught up in rhythm's thrall

Impossible to tell where I ended
and where he began, but it did end
It ended when he said…
"Scott, with you it's all or nothing,
and I can't give all."

He married someone else…
someone who didn't require…
or perhaps need all
And I married someone who…
was an all around good guy

So we went our separate ways…
dancing to different beats
Denying the song in our hearts…

And My Heart Is Dancing Alone

me crying in my sleep
Funny how you can dance alone…
even when your heart and soul is gone

But you never forget a favorite song…
the way it made you feel
The way you danced… the steps you learned,
the hunger not since filled
Others come and others go…
but no song can match lost bliss

For close to thirty years…
my heart danced alone… like this
Then in July of 2005…
the music came alive

Although we lived miles apart…
I found him by my side
His possessions packed in a moving van…
across the country he drove
From Ohio to California…
he traveled the dangerous road

He left his family, his friends, his home…
on US… to take a chance
At last our hearts would beat as one…
at last our souls would dance

For two short years… our life together…
was feverish and sweet
We spent our time… learning how to dance…
both on and off our feet

STILL GROWING

Giving and taking… taking and giving…
We laughed, we dreamed, we argued and cried
We pledged a lifetime of being together…
at each other's side

How could it end the way it did…
so unexpectedly?
How could he leave…
in the middle of the dance?
How could he leave without me?

On March 19, 2007… at 11 P.M.
my soul's mate, my rock…
my heart's true flame
Danced off alone into eternity,
away from all life's pain

Yet through all my tears… my two left feet
and my heart… that sometimes skips a beat,
I can't say that I'm unhappy
Devastated and broken hearted—yes,
but not unhappy

Everything considered…
I'm pressing on… with my life
My only regret is… now there's no chance…
I'll ever be his wife

And once again… I find my heart…
Dancing Alone.

2

BABY BOY

***For My Second Born
Extraordinary Son***

I'm extremely proud of my baby boy
who is now a conscious grown up man
Unlike those who only talk a good game,
he constantly does whatever he can

To live each day by the values
many others loudly profess
Knowing someone will find fault
even when he does his very best

He's not just my son
He's a brother, father, uncle and a friend
Who respects, supports and empowers
his associates as if they were kin

He's also a philosopher, a professor,
a prophet and a priest
Reclaiming ancestral wisdom
and sacred mysteries of the East

*No matter how much love I have
for my Baby Boy,
Who to this day continually fills me
with wonder, pride and joy*

STILL GROWING

That love is dwarfed by the enormous
respect I have for the man
Who is committed to the reemergence
of life's mystical plan

He is ensconced in my heart
and forever will be,
The extraordinary man child
who was entrusted to me.

3

BLUE STAR BLESSING

***For Allison Who Brought
a Special Blessing to Me***

It happened on a mild, gray,
slightly overcast day
That a Blue Star Blessing
came flying my way
The angel who bore it
had large brown round eyes
And a sparkling silver black crown
of diminutive size

The illumination from her spirit
was breathtaking to behold
It was immediately evident
this was a heaven sent soul
The Blue Star she held was pulsating
and glowed from within
I was overwhelmed by its blessing
as she placed it on my skin

How perfect the joy,
the peace and the love
When you happen to be sent
a Blue Star from Above
Thank you My Angel.

4

GONE FISHIN'

For the Family of Newton Amison
Bowers: 6-11-39 to 11-19-09

Gone Fishin'
is what the note simply read
No longer look for me
imprisoned in this bed

I put on my boots
and I walked away
I've gone to catch some fish
and enjoy a brighter day

A day filled with wonder
and sparkling blue streams
Overflowing with fish
even bigger than I dreamed

I'll spend all day fishing
and night will never come
I'll take comfort in the river's
unending tranquil hum

There are blue skies ahead
for as far as I can see
And a secret fishing hole
is waiting just for me

STILL GROWING

So I slipped away quite peacefully
a night or so ago
To join the procession
of life's relentless flow

So please don't be sad
cause at last I'm free
To be the fisherman
that I was meant to be

I've gone fishin'
over on Jordan's shore
And that's where you'll find me
fishin' for ever more.

5

HE'S THE ONE

*For Siyolo, the Son Who
Always Brings Me Happiness*

No doubt about it, he's the One,
the one and only one
Who happens to be my very favorite
first born son

HE was for his parents, a child
much anticipated
And whose birth his big sister
eagerly awaited

For her he was a playmate,
companion and wonderous sight
Her first question,
"Mama, Is this Baby White?"

To this she replied,

*"Black comes in numerous shades
from darkest dark to lightest light"*

*"In truth, Black involves a lot more
than what can be observed
by human sight"*

STILL GROWING

In a short time, he became
a proud big Brother
And for many years it was impossible
to tell one brother from the other

These days it's apparent to all
that he's the one
Who is Marching to the beat
of his ancient ceremonial drum

A caring, helpful
and ancestral soul
Spreading love, happiness and joy
his continual goal

Providing for his family
with all the means at his command
Constantly making himself available
to lend a helping hand

Insuring his old blind mother
never suffers from neglect
Always caring for her with honor,
love and respect

No doubt about it, he's the One
The one and only one
Who happens to be my very favorite
first born son.

6

I AM

An Affirmation for Myself

I am Old, Black and Blind
Non judgmental, Loving and Kind
Confident, courteous and fancy Free
And no doubt about it,

I Really Like Me

I Am Helpful, Supportive and Eloquent
Optimistic, Independent and Intelligent
Outgoing, Creative and Friendly
And You Can Just Bet,

I Really Like Me

I Am Not Argumentative, Petty
or Disrespectful
Egotistical, Greedy or inflexible
Abusive, Selfish or Nasty
All Things Considered,

I Really Like Me.

7

JUST BECAUSE

The Music Started Playing and the Dancing Began 64 Years Ago Today

64 years
of both days and nights
768 months
of both wrongs and rights
3,328 weeks
of doing the things that everybody does
And I'm loving it all…
just because

This life of mine
though old is new
And at 64,
I dance however I choose
I've started over more times
than I can count
And though often knocked down,
I've never been out

64 years
of both goals and dreams
23,725 days
of both plans and schemes
569,400 hours

STILL GROWING

of dancing with family and friends
To an ageless song
that never ends

Creating a lifetime
of memories so great
That I'll be dancing
far beyond this life's gate
But for now I'm here and dancing
like you never saw
And loving every dance step…
just because

64 years
of both bright skies and haze
34,164,000 minutes
of both thanks and praise
2,049,840,000 seconds
of living much longer than some
And I'm excitedly anticipating
the music to come

Having danced quite furiously
for 64 years
I've learned to appreciate
both the joy and the tears
This dance called life
fills me with gratitude and awe
And after 64 years,
I love it all…

just because.

8

JUST CALL ME SCOTT

An Affirmation for Myself

There are some who call me poet
There are a lot who call me friend
There's only one who calls me lover
And many who call me kin

I've been called by various names
But none ever seemed to fit
Some lasted for a number of years
Many for just a bit

I was Scott
since the time I can remember
Scott since the day I could stand

Whether you think it's fashionable
Or whether you think it's not
Until I regain my true family name
let it be known
That all should call me Scott.

May 7, 2012

9

KISSING

For Caple Young
September 17, 2020

Many, many years ago,
when I was oh so young
There was a boy I loved to kiss
Though never with the tongue
He was tall, dark, handsome
and oh so very sweet
For hours we'd talk and kiss
while sitting atop the stairs
On the corner of
San Pedro and 92nd Street…

Now that I'm an old woman
And my eyes no longer see
The young boy who I loved to kiss
Is yet a friend to me
Though we rarely see each other
And our lips no longer meet
He sends homemade cookies in the mail
delicious, moist and sweet

Reminding me of evenings spent
atop the stairs on the corner of
San Pedro and 92nd Street.

10

LIBATION FOR OUR ANCESTORS

In Praise of the Ancestors … You Who Brought Me to This Place, This Time, This Consciousness
January 1, 2009

Although your bodies arrived
in the belly of the slavers' ships
Your souls always dwelled
beyond the chains and whips

For you I pour out a cup
and boldly say,

**"We will never forget…
For you ASHAY"**

For you whose bones lie
on the bottom of the ocean deep
Upon your flesh
the great sharks did feast

For you I pour out a cup
and boldly say,

**"We will never forget…
For you ASHAY"**

STILL GROWING

For the brethren and kin
whose names I may never know
Your blood like rivers
in the Americas did flow

For you I pour out a cup
and boldly say,

**"We will never forget…
For you ASHAY"**

For our warriors who fought
despite overwhelming odds
Sacrificing their lives
for our freedom's cause

For you I pour out a cup
and boldly say,

**"We will never forget…
For you ASHAY"**

For the mothers whose babies
were torn from their breast
And sold for profit stored
in white America's chest

For you I pour out a cup
and boldly say,

**"We will never forget…
For you ASHAY"**

For the field hands who toiled

Libation for Our Ancestors

from the crack of dawn
It's your backs great economies
were built upon

For you I pour out a cup
and boldly say,

**"We will never forget…
For you ASHAY"**

For my stolen people
who were stripped to the bone
Of our language, our religion,
our culture, our home

For you I pour out a cup
and boldly say,

**"We will never forget…
For you ASHAY"**

For the conductors who navigated
the stars and the moss
Leading our people out of enslavement
and off the cross

For you I pour out a cup
and boldly say,

**"We will never forget…
For you ASHAY"**

For all our martyrs
who made the ultimate sacrifice

STILL GROWING

While knowing full well
their life was freedom's price

For you I pour out a cup
and boldly say,

**"We will never forget…
For you ASHAY"**

For you who were lynched,
castrated, brutalized and defiled
For every black woman,
man and child

For you I pour out a cup
and boldly say,

**"We will never forget…
For you ASHAY"**

To our African ancestors,
you are heroes all
For it's on your shoulders
that we now stand tall

So for all of you I pour out a cup
and boldly say,

"We will never forget…

We will never forget…

We will never forget…

For you ASHAY."

11

LITTLE SISTER

***She Always Greeted Me by Saying:
"Here Comes Somebody, Who Looks
Just Like Somebody, I Love."***

And I knew ... in me
she saw her little sister
The little sister
with the huge brown eyes

The one born three months
before their mother died
The mother little sister never knew
but for whom she often cried

Nine children, left alone,
age ten and under
Five big boys, two girls, little sister
and her twin brother

Growing up, like me,
without the love of their mother
Nine siblings struggled
to take care of each other

Little sister was a child
full of both wonder and fear
Many times she found herself...

STILL GROWING

sent here… then there

In time she was convinced…
it didn't matter, she didn't care
And so she decided no one
would be allowed to ever get near

Being afraid of the dark,
little sister always slept with a light
She lived "up in the country"
where creatures roamed in the night

She lived for the day
when she could up and take flight
Far from prying eyes, far from her home
and far out of sight

High school completed,
at last her chance to be free
Off to college she went
with pride and much glee

Only to return in two years,
as pregnant as could be
Returning to the small town
where every eye could see

Little sister, now eighteen,
went from sister to brother
Giving birth to a girl baby
she passed on to another

When the gossip and stares

Little Sister

she could stand no further
She boarded a train
and left her home town border

All total she had three children,
the oldest a girl
But her first born son
was the only light in her world

No loving deeds or words
for his big sister or little brother
Just go to school, go to church,
do your chores and mind your mother

My mother and I,
our relationship was never close
We lived in the same house
but I felt like a ghost

We never spent time
doing anything I chose
And right after high school
I left, I hit the road

"You remind me of somebody"
her big sister said to me
"You look like my little sister
who grew up quite beautifully"

I knew she meant well
but the resemblance I didn't see
After all her little sister
was always a mother to me.

12

MY LIFE REVOLVES AROUND ME

*Life's the Dance We Learn and
I'm Still Learning to Dance*

I'm single, unattached
and free as the breeze
I come when I want
and go where I please

My primary concern
is my own personal needs
My life these days
revolves around me

I earn my own money
and pay my own way
And when it comes to decisions,
I'm the one with the say

No arguments, no drama,
no hell to pay
It's all about me
each and every day

I get up at my leisure,
no breakfast to make

STILL GROWING

I rarely cook
and even more seldom bake

I eat alone or go out
for a lunch or dinner date
My gratification's the only thing
being served on my plate

My radio is programmed
for rhythm and blues
Some funk, some jazz
and sometimes the news

I keep it down low,
kind of mellow and smooth
No loud raunchy lyrics
interrupting my groove

I don't have to watch sports
or reality TV
Forensic Files and Cold Case
are the programs for me

I like blood and gore
and unsolved mystery
These days I choose to watch
what I want to see

It doesn't matter on which side
of the bed I sleep
I can sprawl out all over
or roll up in the sheet

My Life Revolves Around Me

I like my cover soft as down,
my mattress firm as concrete
And on cold nights I wear socks
to warm up my feet

My closet is small
but now it's all mine
I can use all the best hangers
and I like that just fine

No clothes on door backs
or in the garage on a line
And I can find what I look for
each and every time

I buy sexy lingerie
for my own selfish delight
And when I look in the mirror
I appreciate the sight

These days it only matters
that I like what I like
And these days I like being
in control of my life

I remember a not too distant time…
when none of this was true
When all my days were spent…
sharing everything with you

I wasn't I, but rather WE,
and we always knew
That whatever life sent our way…

STILL GROWING

it would be shared by two

In no way did I ever think…
that we would become just me
That my life wouldn't revolve…
around the WE that had come to be

I wasn't prepared to flip the script…
I didn't want to be free
I never wanted to have my life…
revolve around just me

There was no vote, I had no voice;
the decision wasn't mine
Although I've been forced to dance alone
I know I'll be just fine

I'll always miss the life I had,
the love I left behind
But every day looms bright and clear
and I'll be OK in time

Nowadays there's no doubt…
that I hold the key
I've unlocked the doors to my heart
and so it's dancing free

That I'm doing my thing…
it's impossible not to see
How my life these days,
revolves around just me.

13

PERFECT

The Importance of Practice

Practice makes perfect,
when young, we were told
But as for me Perfect
is not a desirable goal

In reality, how long
does Perfect actually last
Perhaps A second or two
and then it is past

If I had to sustain Perfect,
I'd be bored to death
Because once I achieved Perfect
what goal would be left

Practice generates improvement;
which is the goal I desire
And improved performance is something
that everyone can admire

Practice may not make perfect
as we were once told by adults
But, no doubt, Practice will definitely
improve performance and results.

14

REAL BLACK MEN

I love you Black man
in every hue
From pale white ecru
to ebony blue

I'm not impressed by your dick size,
deep pockets or ride
Honesty, loyalty and fidelity
are the qualities I prize

Standing straight and proud
you may be only four foot two
But there are many six-foot men
who are not as tall as you

You know those fellas
whispering in every woman's ear
Telling a broken hearted story
that's never quite clear

Breath and britches I call them,
always hanging out with his boys
No time for a relationship
but always making noise

STILL GROWING

About how he happens to be
every woman's dream
Saying things like, "Girl, you look
like you should be with me"

Their primary interest
is in a woman's cooking skills
For them cooking in the kitchen
and bedroom is what seals the deal

No real commitment
no thought of her needs
Conversation just long enough
to get what they please

Then it's off to the next
and the next after that
Always talking about
how all Black sisters are whack

A real Black man is someone
who doesn't boast or brag
He is confident not cocky
and you would never see him sag

He provides for his woman
all the things that she needs
Sharing more than his body,
he shares her aspirations and dreams

His word can be relied upon,
his actions above reproach
His family, friends and education

Real Black Men

are the things he values most

Real Black men know the difference
between a house and a home
They are available to their children
wherever they roam

Real Black men work to keep their partner
safe, satisfied and secure
Building the type of relationship
guaranteed to endure

They are positive role models,
examples for everyone they meet
Always Striving to do better himself;
yet mentoring the man on the street

Real Black men don't have the need
to be the one who's always right
They see the world in countless shades
not only in black and white

And they don't have to be the super star,
just a member of the team
Real Black Man
you are A TRUE BLESSING

You're the answer
TO EVERY Black woman's dream
And by your side is where every
strong Black woman longs to be seen.

15

REVELATIONS OF A STOLEN CHILD

Look At Me, See Who I Am
For I Am A Stolen Child

From my mother's womb
I was surgically excised
And about my biological,
I was constantly lied

They didn't want you,
they sold you for beads
They couldn't take care of you
or see to your needs

You had better be happy
that we took you in
Otherwise you'd be a savage
just like your kin

Your surrogate family
is as good as gold
It's these kinds of lies,
when young I was told

Never mind that I was always
treated with disdain

STILL GROWING

That I always wondered what
was my true family name

How I often saw others
who looked just like me
Bloodied, mutilated, charred
and swinging from a tree

Never mind that my schools
were never the best
And I had to excel
just to pass the simplest test

And still I was told,
look how lucky you are
You live in a place where
you can reach for a star

Go ahead reach for the stars,
you surrogate child
And though your way is blocked,
just maintain a smile

Keep on smiling
and dance a fancy jig
That's what's expected
of our stolen "nig"

You can have what's left over
whenever we're through
So you had better be glad
that we care about you

Revelations of a Stolen Child

That you're our child,
it's quite easy to tell
As surrogate parents, we bred
and trained you real well

So what if for you,
the jobs are not there
I hope you don't think
that your surrogates care

For generations we slaved
in the hot sun for free
Ensuring enormous wealth
for Europeans' family tree

These days their children's children
are reaping the rewards
Of our ancestor's blood,
sweat, tears and unpaid toil

Don't fret stolen one,
your reward lies ahead
You can surely collect it
once you're good and dead

Just as sure as day follows
each and every night
The universe is destined
to make all things right

The child who was stolen
while still unborn
Who was raised in the west,

STILL GROWING

the subject of ridicule and scorn

Looked in the mirror to see
her true mother's face
Confirming her stolen
African history and race

We American Africans
and all stolen ones
Now stand on the threshold
of an amazing dawn

As we reclaim our heritage
and legitimate birth right
Must continue the struggle
and freedom's fight.

16

SHE IS

For THANAYI ANANA
October 19, 2011
Happy 48th Birthday

Today she is becoming
what I knew she was born to be
A beautiful and elusive butterfly;
a mystical majesty
She is soft and gentle,
a child of happiness and dismay
Moving forward in a crooked line
Facing the past with each new day

In the safety of her cocoon,
she came to understand
That nature only provides us
with a portion of life's plan
Our true worth and character
result from things we learn
As we confront life's trials
and dilemmas at each turn

Because of her unyielding desire
to persevere and grow
She emerged from her cocoon
radiant and aglow

STILL GROWING

A phenomenal black butterfly;
this mystical majesty
Born to live a sankofa life;
an example for all to see…

She was the first child
born to me…
So life for her
was never easy…
I'm very proud of the woman
she has come to be…
She is my child of happiness;
She is Thanayi.

17

SO WHAT

For Me and Vivie and
All Dreamers 10/11/20

So what

If I'm a hopeless romantic
Living life vicariously
Sporting my rose colored glasses
Ensuring love is all I see

So What

if when I hear a love song
As my heart takes flight and soars
I imagine myself
Wrapped in your loving arms
As we dance across the floor

So what

If I believe in fairy tales
And encounters of all kind
Especially those
with you and me together
Enjoying life sublime

So what

STILL GROWING

if I hang horse shoes
Over each and every door
Cup side up, so our good luck
Doesn't run out on the floor

So what

if I believe that Birthday Wishes
Really do come true
And my most fervent desire is
That my love is shared by you

So what

if I cry when watching movies
Engaged in every scene
Knowing only a happy ending
Is acceptable to me

So What

if all my dreams and wishes
Never do come true
Then all I can say is

SO WHAT.

18

STRONG BLACK WOMAN

An Affirmation for
All My Sisters Everywhere
Never Loose Sight of Self

Today I am celebrating
the undeniable fact
that I am a strong Black Woman

Neither requiring nor seeking
validation from any being other
than from the God within…

therefore I have tossed aside
the shackles of the neo slave master;
the baubles, bangles and rings

that masquerade as evidence
of true love and commitment…
shackles designed to hold me
in a game I can never win

I am a strong Black Woman
and I refuse to be controlled
by the self-serving desires of males

STILL GROWING

who seek only personal gratification;
those who strive to pimp my mind,
my time,my emotions and my life

They are guilty of committing
the ultimate sin… I am strong
by design and strong by desire….

The strength of the ancestors
is infused in every cell of my body
and I cannot, I will not deny

or dishonor them…
Black queens ruled nations;
the least I can do is not allow myself

to be ruled by males who are
merely breath and britches unworthy
of being referred to as real men

We, my sisters, are strong Black Women;
we are the mothers of creation
and the daughters of kings,

for generations we have been
the keepers of the Black family
and home; we are sisters to the moon,

each of us reflecting the majesty
and glory of God; we are the tie
that unites humanity with divinity
from beginning to end

We are strong Black Women

Strong Black Woman

and we must choose not to be victims,
defeated by the misusers
and abusers of the world

We must realize and appreciate
our own worth, the uniqueness
of our black beauty, our indispensable
place in eternity…

We are strong because we must be strong
in order to compliment
the Black Man who demonstrates
the true attributes of real strength

and is comfortable in his own skin,
one who is both capable and worthy
of being a companion, a lover, a partner

and a friend, proudly proclaiming
that the woman he chose for his mate
is a Strong Black Woman.

19

THANKFUL

Being old and single and blind,
There's something I've been thinking about a lot
For instance, All the things I'm thankful for,
which includes the things I'm not

First of all, I'm extremely thankful
to be an old woman who
That During my lifetime, I'VE done a lot
and still HAVE a lot more to do

I'm thankful for ALL my children, each ONE
precious and undeniably unique
Every single day, they manage to make my life
an unexpected treat

And I'm truly thankful that I've learned
some things these seventy plus years
Making it unnecessary that I continually
cry so many tears

Tears about the true love so long passed away
Leaving me a single woman until this very day
Most of all, I'm thankful that I don't need sight to see
that life CONTINUALLY offers infinite possibilities

STILL GROWING

To share WITH OTHERS happiness,
success, JOY and positivity

And my rose colored glasses, though cracked,
haven't failed me yet
So I'm thankful All these things combined
to make me realize that I am truly blessed.

20

THE LOVE UP IN HERE

For All My Brothers and Sisters…
If You Can Hear My Voice or Read These Words…
That Means This Poem Is for You

There's so much love up in here;
I can cut it with a knife
So come on everybody
and get yourself a slice

It tastes like chocolate covered caramel,
butterscotch delight
Guaranteed to thrill your soul
with each and every bite

There's plenty for us
and there's plenty to share
So be sure to take some with you,
when you get up out of here

The mood up in here
is like a Sunday morning groove
When church bells are a ringing
but you're too laid back to move

All the folks are listening
and there's nothing you need to prove
Cause the message from the mic

STILL GROWING

is guaranteed your soul to soothe

It's not about religion
just the stirrings in your soul
Acceptance, love and unity,
each more precious than pure gold

The smell up in here
is just like jasmine in full bloom
It permeates the air
and fills every corner of the room

Whether blooming in December
or in the month of June
It never blossoms too late
and it never blooms too soon

It wraps me in its fragrance
so sensual and so sweet
It makes my spirit jump
for joy every time we meet

The feeling up in here
is like the sweetest lover's touch
It's the kind of thing it seems,
there's never quite enough

The sensation is so thrilling,
it satisfies so much
For all of us in need of stroking…
spoken word is the stuff

It fills up all the empty spaces

The Love Up in Here

and flows all around
It makes me want to jump right in
and frolic till I drown

The sound up in here
is the beating of just one heart
It's the universal rhythm
that has been here from the start

I know you hear that primal drum
beating loud and true
From heart to heart, the message is;
one love from me to you

The love up in here
looks just like all of you to me
An overwhelming blending
of our worldwide family tree

The essence of every heart
living in harmony
It's African-Asian-Latin-Caucasian…
Yes love is each of you I see

It's on your face, it's in your walk,
it's oozing from every pore
So don't forget to spread it around,
once you go out the door.

21

TIME TO BE

For John
October 3, 1951-April 28, 1998

I clearly heard the question
as it was being asked
Originating in the future
or perhaps in the past
The voice was familiar;
insistent and kind
The question poised was;
"Is it 'time to be' time?"

The one thing I can state
with absolute certainty
Is I don't think the question
was meant for me
Still it created a dilemma
I sought to understand
Perhaps such an inquiry
is beyond the scope of man

Yet again I heard the voice
melodic and sublime
"I implore you, let me know;
is it 'time to be' time?"

STILL GROWING

It's been said that for every time
there is a season
And with every season
there must surely be a reason
A reason for the question
with it's answer unheard
Seeking understanding
expressed by a single word

Yes or no, was I the one
supposed to decide
Or was the universe listening
and about to reply
Were the ancestors gathered
with one poised to return
And was this reality
not my deathly concern

My baby brother came
and whispered in my ear
I knew it was him though
his face wasn't clear
He slipped through the veil
that divides death from life
Exposing what for most
is kept out of sight

"Is it 'time to be' time?"
were the words that he said
As we held on to each other,
for so long he had been dead
I felt others around us,

Time to Be

I just wasn't sure who
I wanted him to stay longer
but the moments just flew

Like being hit by lightning
I awoke with a start
Sobbing loudly, clutching
my pillow to my heart
Still in my ears the question
rang loud and clear
Is it "TIME TO BE" time
was all I could hear.

March 21, 2011

www.ingramcontent.com/pod-product-compliance
Lightning Source LLC
Chambersburg PA
CBHW062104290426
44110CB00022B/2709